TIME FOR KIDS READERS

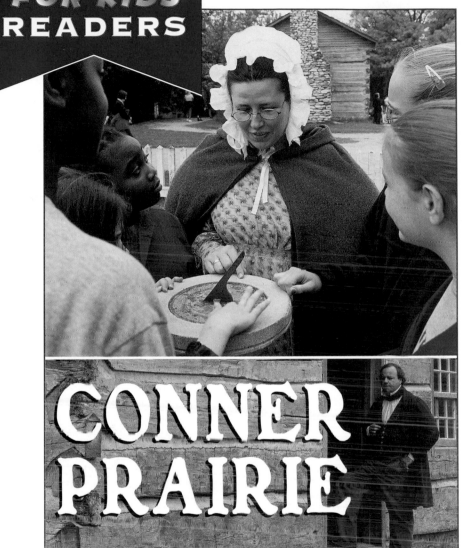

CONNER PRAIRIE

by Edwin Hagonstein

Harcourt

Orlando   Austin   Chicago   New York   Toronto   London   San Diego

Visit *The Learning Site!*
www.harcourtschool.com

INDIANA

• Fishers
★ Indianapolis

Every community should have a leader like Eli Lilly. In 1934 Lilly bought a rundown farm in the town of Fishers, Indiana. The farm's beauty had faded from years of neglect, but Lilly saw its value from the start.

He began to restore the farm. It was a slow process. At the heart of the property was a crumbling two-story brick building constructed in the early 1800s by William Conner. Carefully, Lilly rebuilt it, aiming to restore its original grace.

Once the brick farmhouse was finished, Lilly moved on to other projects. He put up a barn, a log cabin, and a springhouse. A springhouse is a small storehouse built over a cool spring to help keep food fresh. He used traditional designs and materials for each building. Slowly Lilly re-created a farm just as it might have looked 100 years before he bought the property.

This was the beginning of the Conner Prairie living history museum. Eli Lilly's interest in education led him to open his farm to the public. Every year, visitors came in greater and greater numbers. Today, thousands of people from around the world visit the museum at Conner Prairie each year. They go to see firsthand what life was like for early settlers on the Indiana frontier.

Eli Lilly

2

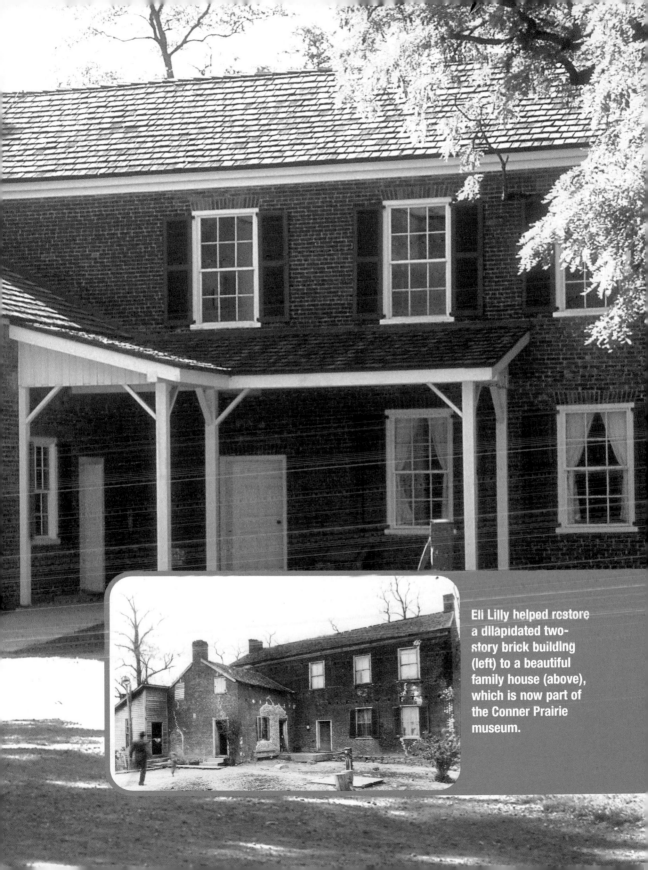

Eli Lilly helped restore a dilapidated two-story brick building (left) to a beautiful family house (above), which is now part of the Conner Prairie museum.

In the late 1700s and early 1800s, thousands of settlers crossed the Appalachian Mountains in search of land to call their own. Many stopped in Ohio, which borders the Appalachians. Many more pushed farther west. In the late 1700s, about 20,000 people lived in what we know today as Indiana. All of them were Native Americans. With more and more settlers moving in, Indiana had a population of 1,500,000 by 1860.

First, hunters and trappers arrived. Almost all of them were men. They opened trails, built crude log cabins, and trapped animals for their fur. They hunted and fished for most of their food. One English visitor described them as "a daring, hardy race of men, who live in miserable cabins. . . . They are unpolished but hospitable, kind to strangers, honest, and trustworthy. They raise a little Indian corn, pumpkins, hogs, and sometimes have a cow or two. . . . But the rifle is their principal means of support."

Settlers eager to build homesteads and raise their families followed these tough loners. A lush landscape awaited them. Once they crossed the mountains, they saw the land rolling out in front of them to the west. This was the interior of North America, a land far from the ocean. An ancient forest carpeted most of what are today the states of Ohio, Indiana, and Illinois. The settlers found flat, grassy prairies there, too. Illinois stopped at the Mississippi River. West of the river, the land gradually climbed again until it reached the mighty Rocky Mountains.

The settlers turned forests into farmland. The summers were hot, and the winters cold. The rich, fruitful Indiana soil kept them alive. The climate, the soil, and the products of the soil were the elements with which the settlers built their new world.

In this broad interior, the settlers built a new world. Their European ancestors may have been peasants, the poorest of farmers, but here in the heartland, the settlers could hope for something better. They could own their own land and farm their own soil.

Before settlers arrived in Indiana, hunters and trappers sometimes lived among the region's Native Americans.

T**EK** 5 Living History Museums

- Plimoth Plantation, Massachusetts, pilgrim life
- Erie Canal Museum, New York State, transportation
- Williamsburg, Virginia, Colonial America
- Washington-on-the-Brazos, Texas, Texas history
- Kona Historical Society, Hawaii, Hawaiian history

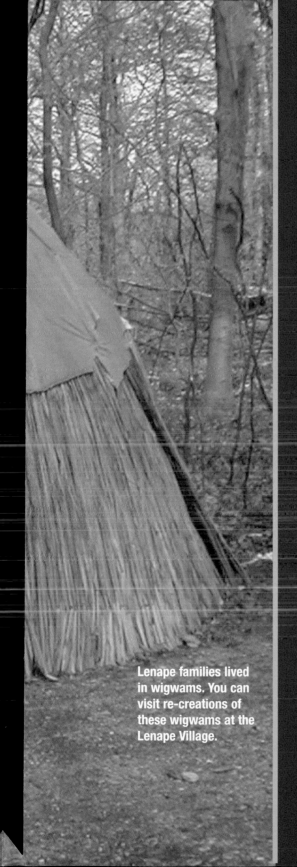

Lenape families lived in wigwams. You can visit re-creations of these wigwams at the Lenape Village.

The history museum at Conner Prairie gives us a living snapshot of the Indiana frontier. Some of the museum's staff dress and work as if they were settlers themselves. They re-create an 1836 farming village, showing how early settlers lived.

The first thing you learn at Conner Prairie is how much the settlers relied on the land. Making a life on the land was always a struggle. The land supplied settlers with most of their food and clothes. They fashioned their tools, wagons, fences, and homes out of trees and stone. Leaves, roots, and tree bark were the source of many of the settlers' medicines. Conner Prairie lets visitors see all the steps that settlers had to take to make items they needed. The living museum lets visitors see how much thought and care it took to live in the wilderness.

Conner Prairie also reminds us that native peoples had lived on this land long before settlers got there. Indiana, after all, got its name because it was once thought of as Native American territory.

One of the displays at the museum is a small Lenape (len•AH•pay) village. The Lenape were among the Native American groups that lived in Indiana during the 1800s. The Lenape village at Conner Prairie looks just as it would have looked in 1816.

The village includes five wigwams. A wigwam was a small structure that Lenape families lived in. The wigwams were made of wooden frames covered with sheets of bark. Wigwams were tied together with vine or other stringy fibers. All these materials were collected from the forest.

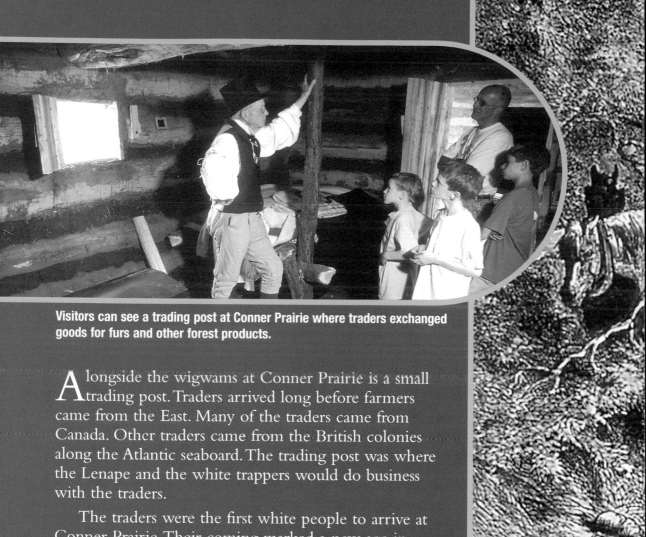

Visitors can see a trading post at Conner Prairie where traders exchanged goods for furs and other forest products.

Alongside the wigwams at Conner Prairie is a small trading post. Traders arrived long before farmers came from the East. Many of the traders came from Canada. Other traders came from the British colonies along the Atlantic seaboard. The trading post was where the Lenape and the white trappers would do business with the traders.

The traders were the first white people to arrive at Conner Prairie. Their coming marked a new age in Indiana, a time when settlers flooded into the territory. This flood of newcomers persuaded the nation's leaders to make Indiana a state in 1816.

Forest still covered much of the region around Conner Prairie at that time. Clearing the woods was one of the first jobs settlers took on. It was also one of the hardest.

Using an axe and perhaps a saw, they cut down the trees. The first clearing they made was for their homes. Settlers used the felled trees to build log cabins. There is an excellent example of a log cabin at Conner Prairie. Next settlers cleared the woods to create fields they could farm on.

Everyone in a pioneer family had chores to do.

The heavy work of clearing the land moved along quickly as more new-comers came. Forests soon gave way to farms. Now the settlers began to rely more on farming for food than on hunting. Conner Prairie museum reflects this change. Farming is at the heart of the museum's displays.

The homesteads that the settlers carved out of the forest were remarkable. Few places on Earth have as much good farmland as the central United States. It didn't take newcomers long to learn that crops grew splendidly here.

Visitors to Conner Prairie watch as corn is hung to dry.

People are invited to grind the corn into cornmeal by hand, just like the original settlers did.

10

Of all the crops around Conner Prairie, corn was king. Corn needs long hot summers and plenty of rain. It also needs fertile soil. It got all three at Conner Prairie.

Today, corn is still one of the most common crops in Indiana. Yet raising corn today is far easier than it was in 1836. Today, Indiana farmers use tractors. Back then, settlers did most of the work by hand. At Conner Prairie and elsewhere in early Indiana, oxen and horses pulled the farmers' plows.

The plows broke the soil in the fields. When an ox pulled the plow, its blades cut into the soil, and the scooped-out shape of the blade helped turn over the soil. The grassy surface also was broken up and turned under. Fresh soil was exposed to the air and sun.

After they prepared the land, farmers planted seeds. The seeds were corn kernels saved from the year before. Seed for other crops were saved the same way. The farmers usually planted corn in May. They could begin harvesting fresh corn late in the summer. They would leave most of the corn on the stalk to dry. Drying made the corn last longer.

People and animals depended on corn to live. It was a big part of the farm family's diet. Settlers ate some of the corn fresh. They ground some of the dried corn into a rough flour called meal. Cornmeal was the staple of the settlers' diet. It could be turned into boiled mush, baked cornbread, or other foods. As you can learn at special dinners at Conner Prairie, settlers even made popcorn.

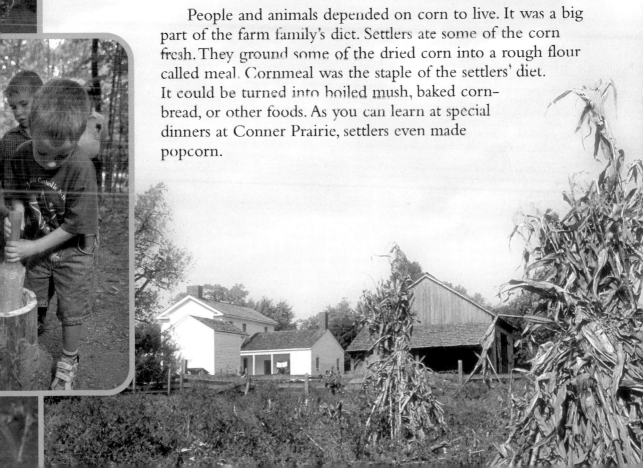

Most of the dried corn was used to feed the animals. One thing visitors notice at Conner Prairie is how many farm animals there were. In the 1800s, farmers raised cattle, sheep, horses, and chickens. They also raised huge numbers of pigs. Indiana today is still a major producer of pigs.

Raised on corn and other crops, these animals, or livestock, were crucial to a farm family's survival. Livestock provided meat and leather. Dairy cows produced milk and cream that could be turned into butter. Chickens furnished eggs, and, of course, oxen and horses pulled plows and other farm implements.

Sheep were important, too. Like cows, sheep provided milk and meat. They also provided wool, a major source of clothing and other goods. At Conner Prairie you can see how farmers turned wool into clothing. A sheep's shaggy fleece, or coat, is made up of long, scratchy hairs—wool. When the sheep's coat gets long enough, the farmer shears off the wool. Today, farmers use electric shears. They buzz through the wool in a flash. Back in the 1800s, the shears were just simple metal clippers, a lot like old-fashioned garden clippers.

"Here's how we spin the wool." Few visitors have seen what's done once wool is sheared.

Once the wool was cut from the sheep, it was cleaned and combed straight. Then it was spun into yarn on a spinning wheel. The spinning wheel twisted the raw wool into a cord, winding up the cord as it formed. Weavers then turned this cord, or yarn, into cloth.

What would the Conner sheep think! A weaver turns their wool into beautiful cloth.

Conner Prairie's staff demonstrates many crafts, and visitors can take classes to learn them. In addition to weavers, you can find a blacksmith, a carpenter, a miller, and others at Conner Prairie. In the small frontier town, all those people provided important goods. The blacksmith, for instance, shaped iron into horseshoes, hardware, wheel rims, and many other items necessary for day-to-day life.

One other exhibit at Conner Prairie completes the picture of the settler's life. This is the display that features a river flatboat. In 1836, flatboats were common on Indiana's rivers. They were flat-bottomed and rectangular. After the growing season, a farmer would often use a flatboat to carry vegetables to market. Indiana's many broad, smooth rivers were perfect highways for flatboats.

No flatboats from the 1830s survive today. One reason for this is that most flatboats were good only for one-way trips. A farmer would build a flatboat and use it to carry farm products downstream. The boats were hard to paddle or sail upstream. To make a little extra profit, the farmers would break up the boats and sell the wood. Then they would walk home.

Building a flatboat—as this man is doing— is a skill demonstrated at Conner Prairie.

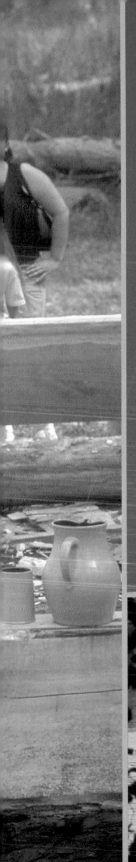

Experts at Conner Prairie built a traditional flatboat from scratch. They used only old-fashioned tools and materials, just as the early settlers had. That flatboat is on display at Conner Prairie. It is kept on dry ground now. Yet it proved to be a sound craft on its maiden voyage in the summer of 2000.

Conner Prairie shows us what life was like in 1836. A snapshot taken just 10 years later would show a very different world. Towns grew and trade increased. Farmers began to hire people to do jobs they used to do themselves. They hired blacksmiths to shoe their horses, and they paid men to float their crops to market. Decade after decade, the villages of Indiana gradually took the shape of those that visitors to the state can see today. The towns changed constantly, and they still do.

Craft Corners at Conner Prairie

Want to go back in time? If so, you'd better learn some old skills. Conner Prairie can help. Its exhibits show you what it takes to

- Be a blacksmith
- Make traditional tools
- Spin wool
- Make pottery
- Use workhorses
- Cook in a fireplace

Rivers were far better than the muddy, rough tracks that passed as roads on the frontiers.

Today Indiana's farmers import machinery and goods from around the world. They no longer float the grain they produce to market. Trains move it hundreds of miles to ocean ports, where ships carry it to countries around the world. Present-day Indiana farmers are less likely to grow their own food than they are to buy it in a supermarket.

There was nothing simple about the lives of the early settlers. They had the same basic needs as people do today—shelter, food, and clothing. Yet they met those needs themselves, day after day, year after year. Conner Prairie shows us how different those settlers were from us—and how alike, as well. The living museum celebrates the people from past generations who helped set the stage for our world today.